tales *of* rural life

Georgia 1938-1946

Joann Hunter Del Re

tales of rural life: Georgia 1938-1946
© Copyright 2018

All rights reserved, including the right of reproduction
in whole or in part in any form.

Illustrations and cover design by
Pamela Jo Hunter

For direct orders, please contact
Joann Del Re at 850-234-8528
or pamelajo56@me.com

Printed in the United States of America

ISBN 978-0-578-20616-5

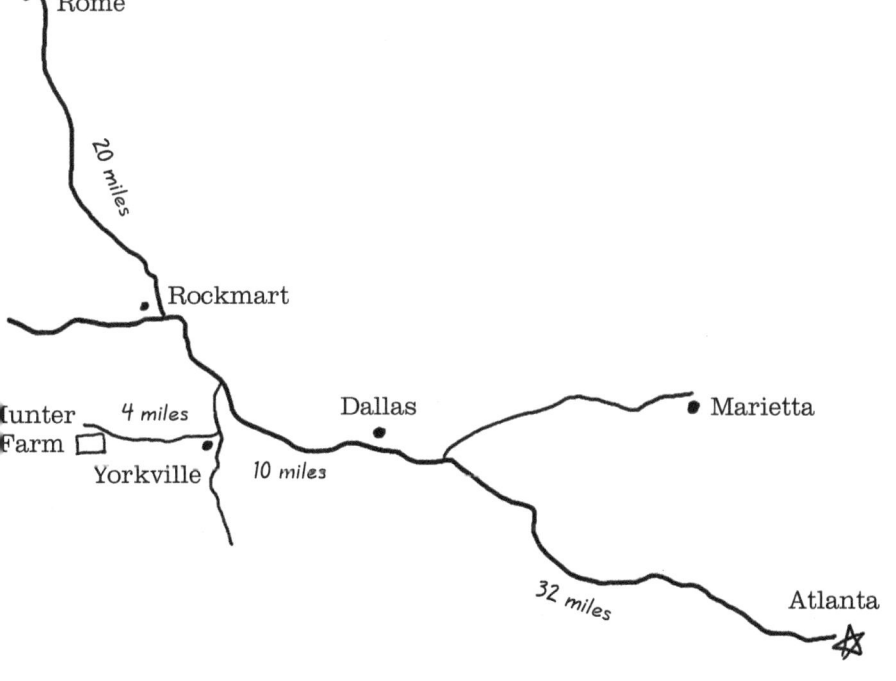

prologue

To those of you who prefer poetry over prose – these "tales" are for you.

To those of you who prefer truth over fiction – these "tales" are for you.

To those of you who read these "tales" – I prefer you.

All illustrations for these "tales" are the creative work of my very special niece, Pamela Jo Hunter (my namesake and the only descendent of my oldest brother, who appears often in these "tales").
A million thanks to her for the artwork, plus her interest and encouragement throughout my little endeavor!

And to my sister, Sandra Hunter Buckland (who literally appears in "tale three"), I give the credit for this venture. Had she not told me I should write a book about our rural life, I'm certain you wouldn't be reading these "tales." A heap big <u>thank you</u> to her!

about the writer hereof

I was born in Rome, Georgia, in 1932. I began my eight years of "rural life" in 1938. In 1946, I left to enter The Martha Berry School for Girls in Rome. After graduation in 1949, I attended business college in Birmingham, Alabama, and two years later, moved to Atlanta.

In 1965, I moved to San Francisco, married in 1972, and retired in 1976. My husband and I were transferred to Atlanta in 1983, then to New Jersey in 1987. He retired in 1997 and we returned to California. When I lost him to cancer in 2005, I moved to Florida to rejoin my family.

I have always loved poetry (and music!) and began writing limericks in 2013.

(All my children have had four legs each and purred!)

tale one

Daddy was left with four children when our mother was taken to Heaven:

Me, aged three months; my two brothers, four and eight; and my sister, eleven.

For the next five years we kids lived mostly with kin,

While Daddy was off "falling in love," and getting married again!

Our new mother was only nineteen when her introduction to us was given.

Daddy was raised in the country and wanted to go back – luckily he soon found a farm for rent.

We piled our belongings into our old pickup truck, hopped in, and off we went!

The house had four big rooms, was old, and had seen its best.

We had only a few pieces of furniture, so Daddy and my brothers built the rest.

AND IT WAS THERE AND THEN
THIS ALL BEGAN –
MY "TALES OF RURAL LIFE"
AS THEY WERE SPENT!!!

tale two

The nearest school was nearly a mile away,

And my older sister and brothers
and I had to walk to and fro each day.

   I never knew why there wasn't
   a school bus,

      It caused such a hardship for all
      of us.

My sister soon left to attend another school when we found friends with whom she could stay.

The closest store was also a mile away, so one thing we were thankful for

Was the arrival each month of what we called the "rolling store."

    We kids knew, of course, there was tons of great stuff

    Just waiting inside for us, if we had money enough!

But the "rolling store" man would swap our eggs for candy, chewing gum and more!

tale three

A few years after moving to the country,
I came home from school one day

And saw a big black car sitting in our driveway.

   Quickly I ran to the door to see

   Who in the world our company could be.

But Daddy came out and softly asked me to stay outside and play.

Pretty soon a man came out of the house, got in the car, and drove away.

Then Daddy called me in, and these words he had to say...

   "Honey, you have a new baby sister!"

   And I cried, "Oh, Daddy, can I please see her?"

She was the first of four to arrive
(a girl and two boys each still awaited its day).

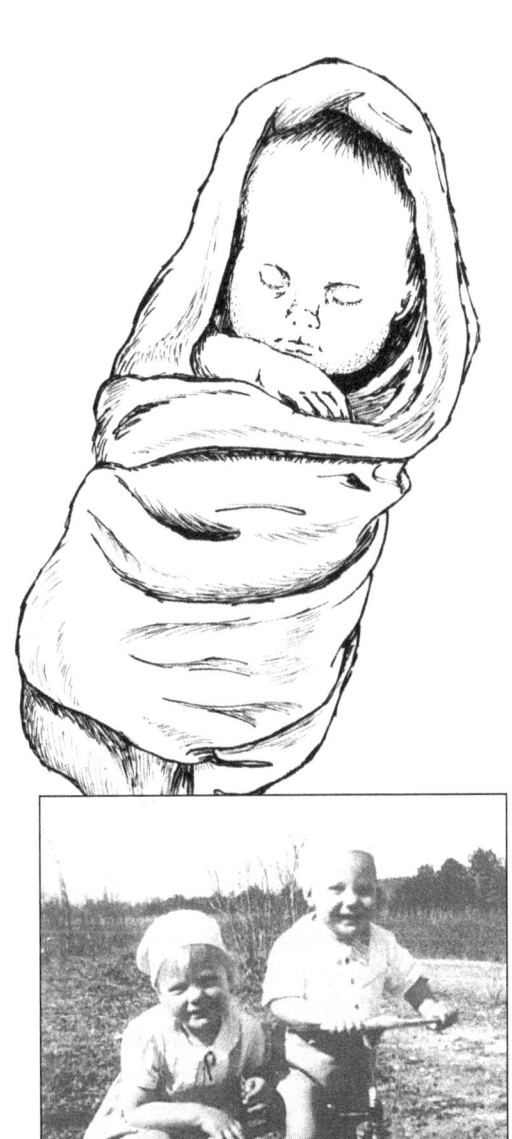

Baby sister and brother

tale four

We had a fairly long driveway with woods on either side.

My brothers built me a playhouse next to it (in which they sometimes liked to hide).

   It had no windows, and just an opening for a door.

   It had a roof of tin, but only dirt for the floor.

(Not exactly an architectural gem – but good enough to fill me with pride!)

One night when we ran out of milk, my brother (who feared the dark) was sent to our neighbor's to borrow some.

He dilly-dallied around with the neighbor's kids 'til it was dark when he headed home.

> Whistling loudly and swinging his bucket of milk, he was nearing the playhouse door,
>
> When my older brother bounded out and yelled with a very deep roar...

"Hey! Watcha got there!" – but he was not ready for the answer that was quick to come...

A pail of milk came flying at his face and little brother was running for home!

When Daddy was told what happened, he realized what had to be done.

> He was a very good man, and he knew when and how to discipline.

> Both boys were taken to the barn and each given a solid lickin'!

For supper that night, we had lots of cornbread, but milk to soak it in – none!

tale five

Our sole means of communication with the outside world was a battery-operated radio.

We could hear the latest news, keep up with the "soaps," and often catch a comedy show.

"Stella Dallas" must have been a favorite "soap" of mine

Because I can still recite its opening line...

"And now Stella Dallas – the true-to-life story of mother, love and sacrifice in which Stella Dallas saw her beloved daughter, Laura, marry into wealth and society..." and on it would go.

The show the whole family liked best was "The Grand Ole Opry" every Saturday night.

We'd gather round the radio, tune in WSM, and just listen, by our old kerosene lamp's soft light.

There'd be Minnie Pearl exclaiming "Howdy, I'm so proud to be here";

Hank Snow (movin' on!), Roy Acuff, Ernest Tubb and many others we held so dear.

When the "Opry" ended, we'd blow out the lamp, crawl in bed under our hand-made quilts, and sleep tight!

tale six

During those sharecropping years, our major crop was a big cotton field.

We shared the labor with the landowner in return for a share of the yield.

   The cotton was usually ready for picking in early Fall,

   And needed to be picked quickly, so all hands were on call.

If heavy rains were to come, the cotton could get splattered with mud or become spilled.

Everybody who could help carried a big burlap sack

And plucked the cotton from each boll, walking between the rows, up and back.

> We emptied the sacks of cotton into a high-bed truck, and then
>
> When the truck was full, we kids would climb up on top and "float" off to the cotton gin.

The gin removed all debris and seeds, packed the cotton into huge bales and rolled them out on a track.

We usually ended up with seven
or eight bales at the landowner's house,

Until sold, we kids played among
them – games like "cat and mouse."

But picking cotton was very
hard work, especially in the
sweltering hot sun,

Totin' and draggin' the heavy sacks
of cotton all day, one by one.

Not to mention the bleeding fingers
caused by the spikey bolls, and fear of
destruction by the boll weevil – the louse!

tale seven

After several years of sharecropping and living in a rented home,

We bought a large piece of farmland and woodlands of our own.

   No house still existed, but there was a barn.

   A lone chimney was left standing so forlorn.

During the following year, our new house was built by just Daddy and the boys alone.

In the front yard of our new home, beside a dirt road,

Stood two magnificent big trees... a water oak and a hickory nut, both very old.

During the summer the oak provided shade from the blazing sun,

And the hickory seemed to bear nuts by the ton!

There are some folk who've never tasted a hickory nut... or so I've been told.

I decided that was probably true, the first time I tried to eat one!

We had to put a big rock under the tree to lay the nuts on and another rock to use to smash 'em.

We found that a horsehoe nail worked best to dig out the meat.

It was all worth the hassle, for we knew we'd get a special treat!

Our stepmother would put the nuts in her chocolate fudge, and it would be the best in the world, bar none!

tale eight

We regularly attended services at our
local Baptist church,

Where our good ole Baptist preacher
never left us in the lurch!

I joined the church at twelve
years old,

Was baptised in a muddy creek
in water icy cold.

But my pretty homemade dress and I
survived without a smirch.

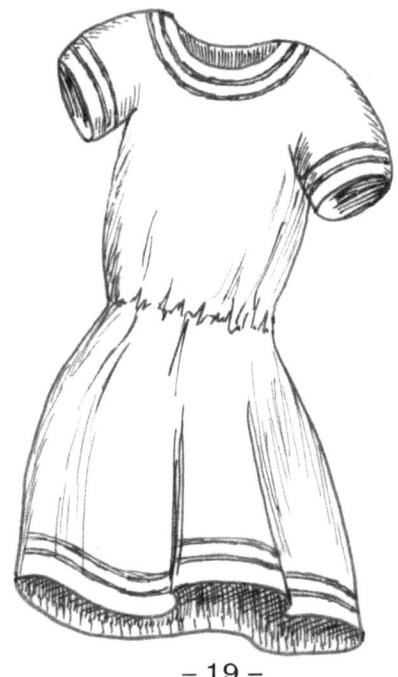

On one Sunday each Spring, our church held an "All Day Singin' and Dinner on the Ground."

Tables were set up outside for food to be brought by folks from all around.

We'd dress up real pretty, grab our food baskets, and head for church at ten.

Popular quartets would sing, off-and-on, all day and we sang in between.

Come noon, we'd all go outside and eat, then go back in and all sing "Amazing grace, how sweet the sound."

tale nine

Our water for drinking and cooking came from a very deep well.

To draw up the water, we used a windlass, rope and pail.

   When the water in the well got low,

   Off to the nearest spring we'd go.

Then swinging our buckets of water, home we'd hightail.

We cooked on a big wood burning stove that had a reservoir,

So there was always plenty of warm water in store.

   The children's daily baths were no rub-a-dub-dub.

   But come Saturday, they washed in a big round tub.

A galvanized one in the middle of the kitchen floor.

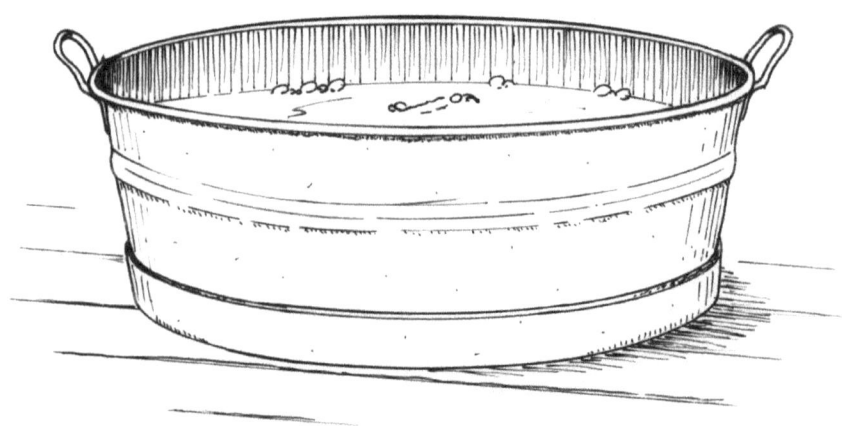

Filling the tub would take all the warm water supply,

While three or four kids waited nearby.

   The youngest got it's bath first, followed by the second, third and fourth,

   'Til all were washed and dried, and preening for all their worth!

I recall all that so vividly... boy, how time does fly!

tale ten

I suppose city folk might have gotten their exercise out hiking on a trail,

But I got a lot of mine from fetching the daily mail.

    Our address was "RFD," to be exact, "Route 4."

    Certain mail routes went just so far, and no more.

Why that was so, no one could tell.

Our route came no closer than half a mile away.

And I didn't mind the trek on a beautiful, sunny day.

    But when the rains came and the road turned to mud,

    I would rather have hidden under the bed, if I could,

And left that ole mail in the mailbox to stay!

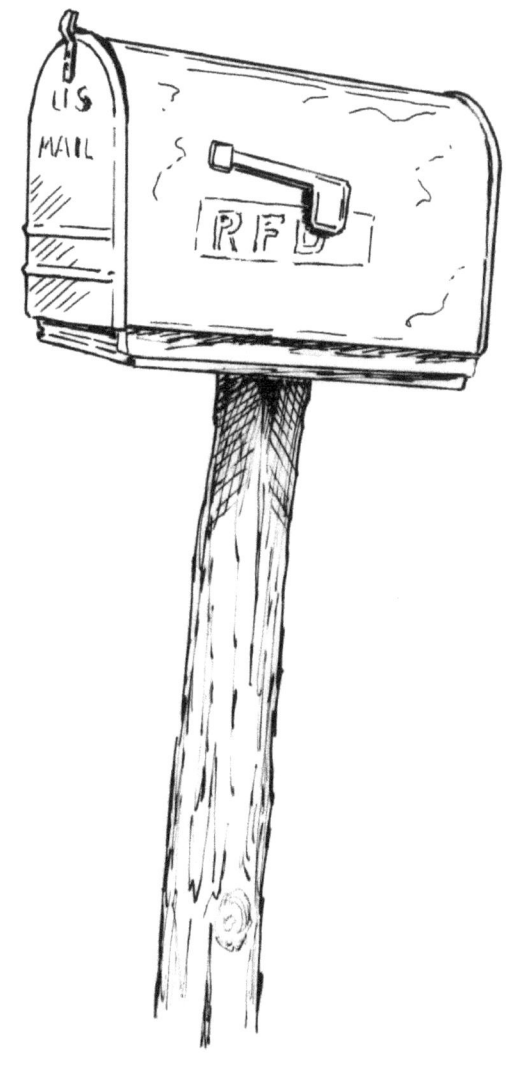

tale eleven

Once when my baby brother was two, he was playing in the yard,

And though he'd been warned not to leave, the warning was ignored!

   And suddenly one day the little guy was gone.

   He was out there somewhere all alone!

We called, searched and walked every road, but not a sound was heard.

Knowing he couldn't have gotten far, we began our search again...

Back and forth on the old dirt roads, calling his name.

Finally, we found him inside a very deep ditch, leaning against the side, sleeping.

He was totally covered in dirt, except for traces of tears from his weeping.

To this day, when I recall that scene, every detail appears exactly the same.

tale twelve

We had no indoor plumbing, so we had an "outhouse" instead.

Our TP was the Sears & Roebuck catalog after it was read.

Mostly, the "outhouse" was peaceful and quiet,

Unless a roving chicken came and reached for a bite!

We'd grab a long stick we kept on hand, swat it, and off it would go "unfed!"

There were many times that Nature would call,

When we were in the barn cleaning a stall.

> Now without any paper, what could finish the "job"?
>
> A red corncob – then a white one to see if we needed another red cob.

When small emergencies arose, we could usually find ways to deal with them all.

tale thirteen

One day each week was "wash day," weather fittin' or not!

We didn't have a washing machine, so we used a big iron pot.

> The pot was filled with water, dirty clothes and soap;
>
> Then a fire was built under it, and the rest was left to hope.

Later, when the clothes were "done," they showed nary a dirty spot.

We rinsed the clothes in a great big tub, then wrung them out by hand.

Our "delicates" we washed separately, using a scrub-board and a pan.

With wooden clothespins, we hung them on the line.

They looked so clean and colorful in the bright sunshine!

All that made for a very rough day, but we could wear clean clothes again!

Back then though, most clothes were made of cotton, so we had to iron the wrinkles out.

We'd fire up our old wood stove and put some irons on top to get hot.

All the clothes to be ironed were sprinkled with water by hand,

Then rolled up in a towel to stand.

When the irons were ready, we'd take turns at the ironing board, each of us sweating and swearing a lot!

tale fourteen

Growing up, the younger of my older brothers was terrified of the dark.

We tried to allay his fear, except his brother treated it as a lark!

   If the little brother needed to "use the yard" during the night,

   Big brother would laugh and make fun of his plight.

So he would wake me up to go with him, my being his last remaining "mark!"

tale fifteen

Of course we had a big cornfield, with so many livestock to feed.

But pulling fodder and shucking corn were not fun chores – no indeed!

   Some of our corn we took to a gristmill to be ground.

   We kids would tag along to see the big wheels go round!

For supper, cornbread in a bowl of fresh milk was all we'd need.

We also grew sorghum cane for making syrup.

Watching the processing at the cane mill was a real "trip!"

　The flow of sweet juice came first,

　And we drank some to quench our thirst.

Then we'd climb the pile of pulp, sit down on our butts and slide down with a zip!

We loved to pop (and eat!) popcorn, so each year we planted a small patch.

With popcorn and a tad of lard in a pot on the stove, we'd pop up a batch.

For a sweet treat, we sometimes made popcorn balls, too...

By heating a little sorghum in a skillet till it was thick like glue,

Then with buttered fingers we used the syrup to form balls! Scrumptious? Natch.

tale sixteen

Owning pigs, cows, mules, etc., in the country is the norm.

But if you own mules, you must have corn.

    Now a mule loves its corn – but
    so does a rat!

    Rats took over our corncrib – so
    how did we deal with that?

My two brothers took care of the problem later one early morn...

After a trek through the woods to check their rabbit traps,

They came home with something slithery in one of their burlaps...

    A real live rat snake about
    four feet long,

    Very big around and very strong.

They locked it in the corncrib and sealed up all the gaps.

We named the new tenant "Charlie," and what a glutton was he!

He spent each night devouring every rat he could see.

During the day he would just lie on a rafter and sleep...

Except to give us corn-shuckers below an occasional peek.

But finally our corncrib was totally rat free!

tale seventeen

Watermelons were probably the most-loved food in our neck of the woods in the Fall.

Every farm had its own watermelon patch, but the theory was "all for one and one for all."

Unfortunately, that theory seemed to apply to the crows, too.

They pecked huge holes in the melons, ate a few bites, and away they flew.

The local kids were somewhat like the crows... they busted the melons, ate only the hearts, and left the rest for the farmer to haul!

tale eighteen

As youngsters working in the field one day,

Around an old stump my brother and I began to play.

    Lo and behold, this very strange critter we found,

    Half-in and half-out of the red clay ground.

It certainly looked like nothing we saw every day!

My brother scooped it up in his old straw hat,

And we raced off home, totin' it like that.

    Daddy flew out of the house to see

    What in the world our problem could be.

When he saw what we'd brought, his sun-burnt face went flat.

Then Webster's old dictionary he duly fetched,

And the facts about our critter upon our brains were etched.

  We were very thankful that Daddy taught us so well,

  That we hadn't messed around with that old scorpion's tail!

Daddy said he was feeling sorta queezy and went behind the barn and retched.

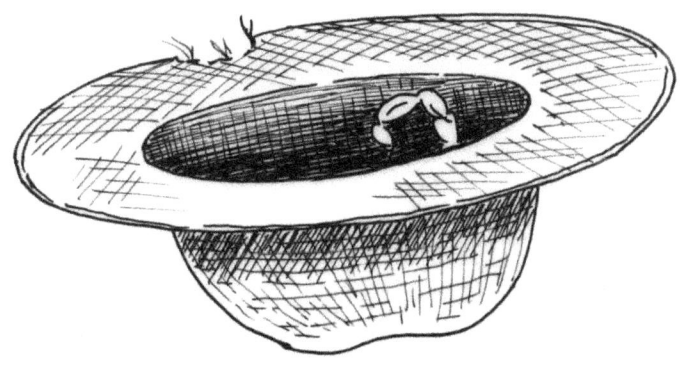

tale nineteen

There were nuisances we dealt with in the country which were not too common elsewhere...

One was the tiny bedbugs which sucked our blood when we were least aware.

> Mornings we'd feel and see
> the signs of their being,

> But not a single hair of them
> would we be seeing.

To kill the bedbugs, our iron bedsteads had to be hauled outside and scalded; bedclothes scrubbed till threadbare.

Another aggravation was the teeny red chiggers from out-of-doors.

They dug holes in our skin and climbed in and itched like crazy for hours.

> The little dudes were fussy
> about where they liked to hide,

> And mostly chose our armpits,
> crotches and navels as places
> to abide.

They were painfully hard to get rid of... we had to cut 'em out, "burn" 'em out, or flush 'em with kerosene pours.

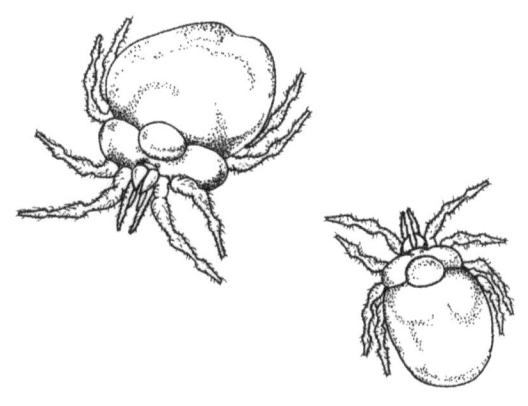

And then there was that most common of all pests – the housefly.

Although we had screens on all our doors and windows, we sometimes wondered why!

> For if we opend a door one inch for one second, a swarm of flies came in.
>
> Quickly we would grab some towels and try to shoo them back outside again.

When we had the money, we'd buy some flypaper ribbons and hang them where the flies would light on them, stick, and die.

Thank goodness, though, most of our little critters didn't annoy,

But often were useful and, all-in-all, were a real joy...

    Like the lightening bugs, butterflies, June bugs, bumblebees and honey bees,

    The katydids singing amongst the trees,

The cooing of the mourning doves, the hooting of the owls, and the lullabyes of the whippoorwills – oooo boy!

The little doodle bugs were lots of fun, too.

They dug funnel-shaped holes for trapping other ants and insects for food.

We'd stir round and round the holes with twigs and utter...

"Doodle bug, doodle bug, come get your supper,"

And they'd come peeking out, as if they understood!

Unfortunately for our June bugs (poor little tykes!),

The boys would catch them, tie strings to their legs, and fly them like kites!

Our lightening bugs fared no better for we girls caught them and put them in Mason jars.

Then from some we took out their little "lights" to make finger rings that shown like stars.

We kids never thought we were being cruel – just having fun and the likes.

tale twenty

My stepmother used to put alcohol (the "rubbing" kind!) on everything...

Which was okay with us kids because it didn't really burn or sting.

One day my baby brother got bit by a chigger on his little "you-know-what."

He toddled into the kitchen, holding it with both hands, tears going "plop."

And lisping, over and over, "Mama, put acacol on it." It was a touching (but funny!) scene.

Daddy was a licensed pharmacist, having completed a course via U.S. mail...

So he had his own home remedies for everything that could possibly ail.

If we ate green apples and got a bellyache, out came the castor oil; for colds, Vicks Rub;

For headaches, baking soda; and sprains got soaked in Epsom salts and warm water in a tub.

But Daddy would only apply his remedies after we described our ailments in detail.

tale twenty-one

A vegetable garden was a huge part of every farm.

We always planted a big one (using fertilizer from our barn!).

   We grew potatoes, carrots, okra, beans,

   Peas, onions, squash, greens,

Cabbage and cucumbers – and lots of tomatoes – and corn.

Tending the garden was no "child's play";
There was something to do every day.

    One job of mine was picking bugs
    off plants by hand

    And dropping them into kerosene
    I carried in an old tin can.

I guess we could have sprayed to kill the
bugs, but Daddy preferred our way.

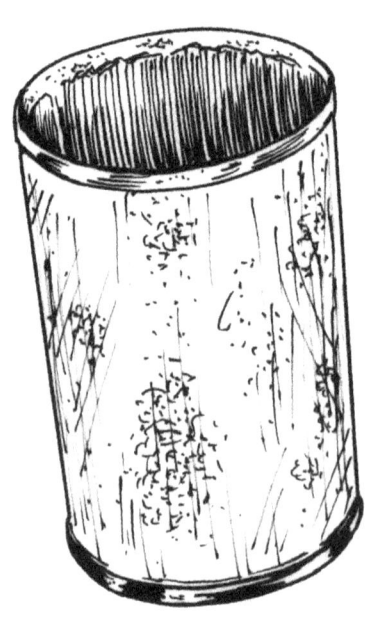

The fruits of our labor and time were enjoyed the year long,

Because we had canned much of everything we'd grown.

    I loved tomatoes, so often I'd grab a cold biscuit and a handful of salt, and off to the garden I'd run.

    And pick a big, red, juicy tomato, still warm from the sun,

Then wipe the dirt off on my overalls, lick the tomato, dip it in salt, take a big bite, and soon it was gone.

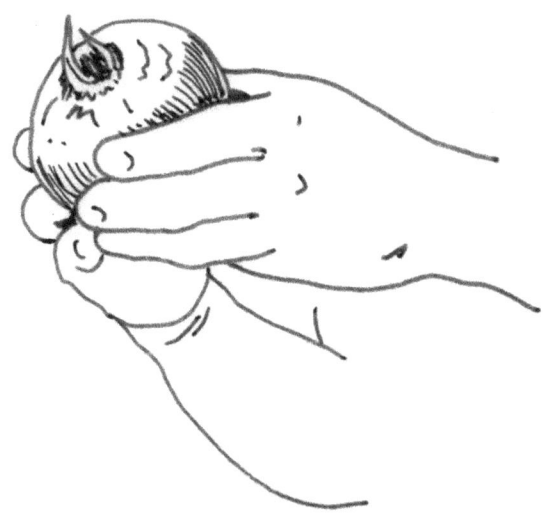

In addition to our garden and a few fruit trees, Nature's bounty was everywhere.

There were blackberries, strawberries, dewberries, and some tiny huckleberry bushes here and there.

   We made lots of jams, jellies, cobblers and pies,

   And I could never decide which enjoyed them more – my nose, mouth, or eyes!

Daddy liked to eat "poke salat" (pokeweed) cooked up like spinach, but I took the berries to paint my fingernails, as my share!

Wild grapes (muscadines) covered several large trees down by our creek.

They were very sweet and juicy – big, black and sleek!

   The skins were so tough, though, we had to bite the grapes, suck out the juice, and toss the skins.

   My brothers climbed the trees to pick the grapes, and came home with skinned arms and shins.

I never knew what wine was until Daddy found out the boys had been making it with muscadines, when they turned up very "sick!"

tale twenty-two

On a hillside in our pasture was a deep fresh-water spring.

We never imagined the tragedy that spring would bring.

One evening a mule was missing from the barn,

So my brother went searching to see had it come to some harm.

He soon found the mule at the bottom of the spring, drowned – poor thing.

First, the mule was pulled from the water (a long and tiresome task);

Then with help from a friend, a huge grave was dug at last.

But "No!" – rigor mortis had set in and the grave was too shallow.

So our friend calmly chopped off the legs and placed them in the grave – (smart fellow).

We could then say good-bye to our faithful servant, while the dirt was being cast.

tale twenty-three

Every rural family owned a good milk cow,

And all untrained in the art of milking were taught how.

Cows must have hated having their tits pulled and yanked that way...

Why else flick their tails in our faces and kick the milk buckets astray?

Without a good cow, though – no sweet milk, no buttermilk, no butter for our grits – no could allow!

There were times though when the milk wasn't fit to drink.

Because Mother Nature wasn't too particular about which plants grew where, I think.

> Our pasture seemed to be her favorite spot for wild onions and bitterweed,

> And upon which plants our cow would often feed.

So we couldn't stand the taste of the milk (and, had we owned one, would have poured it down that proverbial sink!).

Which brings to mind the first time I saw milk in a can!

We got it for our coffee when our milk tasted bad... "Carnation" was the brand.

   Lots of other country folk must have used it, too,

   For a verse was made up about it, which I recite for you:

"Carnation, Carnation, the best in the land.
Here I stand with a can in my hand.
No tits to pull, no hay to pitch,
Just punch a hole in the son-of-a-b - - - -"

It seemed so easy I began to wonder if cows would no longer be in demand.

Without milk and sugar in our coffee each morn,

It would have been too strong to have been borne,

> Because we had to make it by putting ground coffee and water in a pot,

> And setting it on top of our old wood stove to get boiling hot.

Then coffee (with grounds!), milk, sugar and biscuits ("soakie") in a big cup was our breakfast norm.

We always had cats, and they never missed a milking time.

They just seemed to know exactly where and when to dine.

   Each evening they would come
   and sit in their places

   Waiting for squirts of fresh
   warm milk in their faces.

All of us obliged, of course; then licking and blinking, they would leave us behind.

Since cows don't give buttermilk (as everybody knows!),

We'd pour milk into a churn and put a lid on it to close.

    After several days the milk would clabber and cream would form on top.

    Time for me to grab the dasher-and-lid set, for churning was <u>my</u> job.

Up and down, up and down (boring!) 'til clabber turned to buttermilk and cream turned to butter and rose.

tale twenty-four

Halloween was a favorite holiday, with harvesting, canning, hog-killing, and so forth, all done.

It was then time to carve a jack-o-lantern, put together our Halloween costumes, and start planning our fun.

We girls loved to go sernatin (which we later learned was "serenading!") for our treats.

But "boys will be boys," and they would pull tricks of gigantic feats.

Once some trick-or-treaters put our two-horse wagon on top of our barn!!

tale twenty-five

We always knew where Daddy was because he whistled all day long.

Each tune was so cheerful it could have been a lovely song.

    I felt strongly about that because I always loved to sing –

    I even dreamt of becoming famous for that very thing.

I guess fate intervened, because something went wrong!

I kept on singing, though, from a "Hit Parade" magazine that gave words for each song.

My stage was a sawed off tree stump in the woods, and my audience was pine trees by the throng.

   A voice teacher surely would have cringed at the sound,

   But thank goodness there wasn't one around;

Just me, my stage, my audience, and my great desire to sing on!

tale twenty-six

The older of my little brothers could always find something to get into!

Like one day he disappeared and we were trying to decide what to do...

    When out of our kitchen pantry door came this "snow white elf,"

    Who'd found the flour barrel and strewn flour all over "itself!"

Of course every single thing in the pantry was covered in flour, too!

tale twenty-seven

Although work came first on the farm, we did have time to do some fun things:

Like swimming and playing in the creeks and taking quick dips in the cold springs.

> We loved roasting "weenies" and "marsh-mellers" down in the pasture

> Over "the perfect fire" made by my oldest brother who proclaimed himself a "master."

We would tell jokes, each trying to tell the funniest (or the dirtiest!), while watching the fading smoke rings.

Daddy and my two brothers absoultely loved to fish,

And when they got lucky we'd have a tasty breakfast dish.

> My stepmother's squirrel dumplins were ever so fine,
>
> But I'd pass on the baked possum every time.

We had fried chicken every Sunday and each of us kids wanted the pulley-bone so we could make a wish.

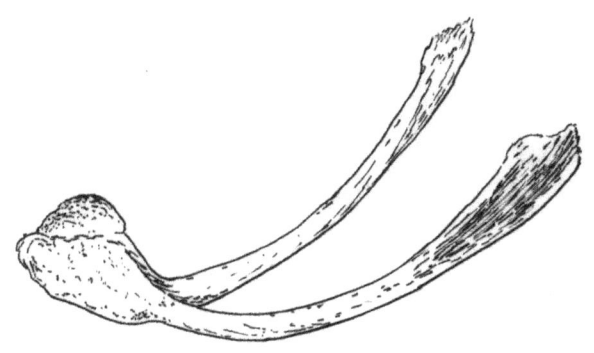

The county fair came to a town near us every year.

We always went for a day of walking, looking, riding, eating, and trying to win every prize there!

> Alas, we would usually get back home, tired and broke,
>
> But maybe clutching a teddy bear to show we'd had good luck.

But no matter – we had all had a great time and were already looking forward to next year's fair.

My brothers built a tree house at the top of a very tall pine.

Getting up there and back was pure h – – –, but once there the view was prime.

    Also, I think they hung swings from every tree they could climb,

    But the swings were all safe and we enjoyed them, so that was fine.

They built see-saws and jump boards, too, so we had fun ways to spend our spare time.

During the winter evenings we would play a lot of checkers, on a homemade checker board.

For checkers we used bottle caps we'd picked up along the road.

   Sometimes after supper, Daddy would tell us ghost stories galore,

   Most of which he made up as he went along, I was sure.

But they were certainly scary enough that we never got bored.

Sometimes Santa would bring me a paper doll book that had extra clothes for the doll (Barbie wasn't born yet!).

At other times I would cut my paper dolls out of the Sears & Roebuck catalog – a whole set:

A mama, a daddy, a baby and a bunch of little kids.

I folded paper to make their chairs, tables and beds.

Then I would talk to them and sing to them, but their silence was all I'd get.

tale twenty-eight

Some of the worst times for us (as well as the rest of the world!) was during the war.

My oldest brother was drafted into the Army and was wounded in action afar.

After spending months in hospitals, he was home again,

Then it was my younger brother's turn – he was sent to Japan.

We younger kids did all we could to help keep the farm up to par.

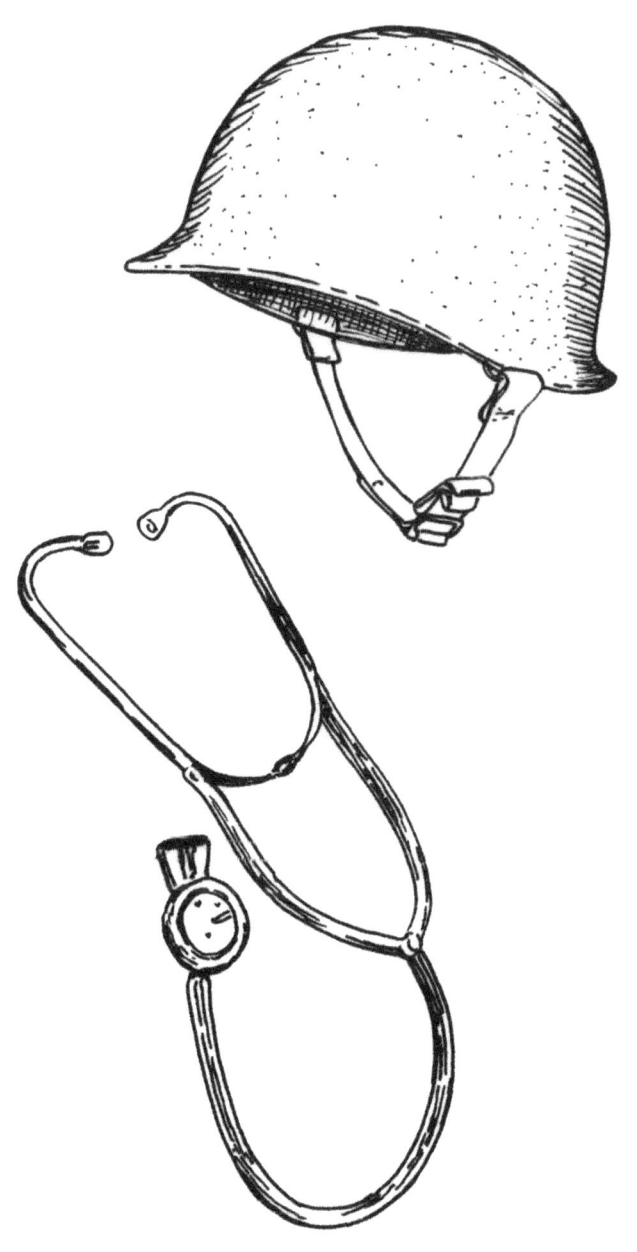

But now with one brother disabled, and the other far away,

Daddy, without their help, had to give up farming and find work with pay.

    After several weeks, he found a job working at a local sawmill.

    Each day I'd watch him trudge down the road carrying his dinner pail.

The work was very hard but he stuck it out 'til he left to work at a cotton mill in town one day.

The town was twelve miles from us, so we'd been there only once or twice.

Now with Daddy working there and making more money, we could go every Saturday – which was nice.

> I particularly wanted to go shopping at the five-and-dime store,

> But going to the picture show (for 12 cents!), I wanted more.

Saturdays they showed cartoons, serials and westerns – Gene, Silver, Roy, Dale, Trigger – and for a nickel we could buy a Co-Cola – with ice!

Another job Daddy held was as a police officer in a very small town nearby.

One evening he came home with a huge watermelon for us to try.

It seems he'd stopped a truck driver (who'd asked what he had done).

Daddy kindly informed him "Your truck is overloaded, Son."

He took off the biggest watermelon he could lift, said "You're okay now," tipped his cap and bid good-bye.

In about 1945, both Daddy and my stepmother went to work in a plant that made the B-29 plane.

On their way to work they'd drop the youngsters with a "sitter" and on their return, pick them up again.

When I got home from school each day, I had beds to make and supper to fix.

The first time I made vegetable soup, I put in so much okra it became a slimy mix!

Everybody gobbled it up anyway – but Daddy was trying so hard not to laugh – I think it caused him pain.

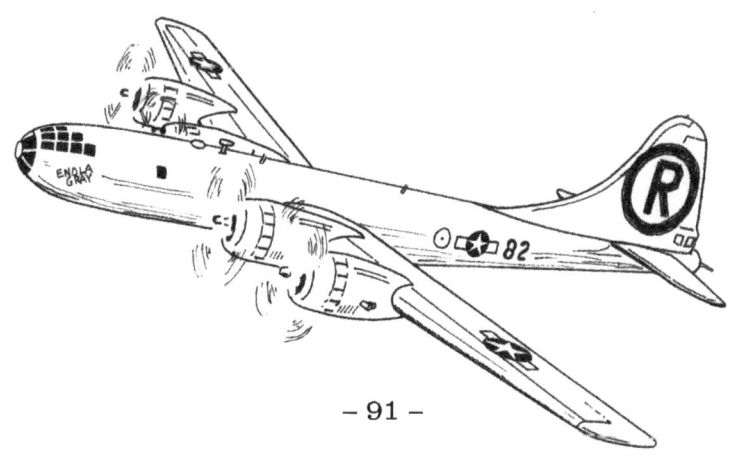

tale twenty-nine

Christmas was always special, particularly for the young,

Because they knew, of course, that's when Santa would come.

And Santa would fill their stockings with goodies galore...

Like oranges, peppermint sticks, chocolate-covered cherries, and more.

And under the Christmas tree they would find presents they asked for in their letters to Santa's home.

Fun for some of us was traipsing through the woods looking for the perfect Christmas tree!

Once found, it was cut down, hauled home, and set up in the front room for all to see.

> We would then cover its base with "snow," which was cotton from our field.

> Then spread more "snow" on all the limbs, as well.

"It is our most beautiful Christmas tree ever!" – we would all agree.

But there was more to be done to beautify our tree, so everybody had work to do.

Money being scarce, we made our own decorations, mostly with paper, and flour-and-water glue.

> We would paste together rings of colored paper into chains to wind all around.

> Icicles were cut from the tin foil inside empty cigarette packs we'd found.

Sometimes we would make pinwheels and bows,and always an angel for the top, too.

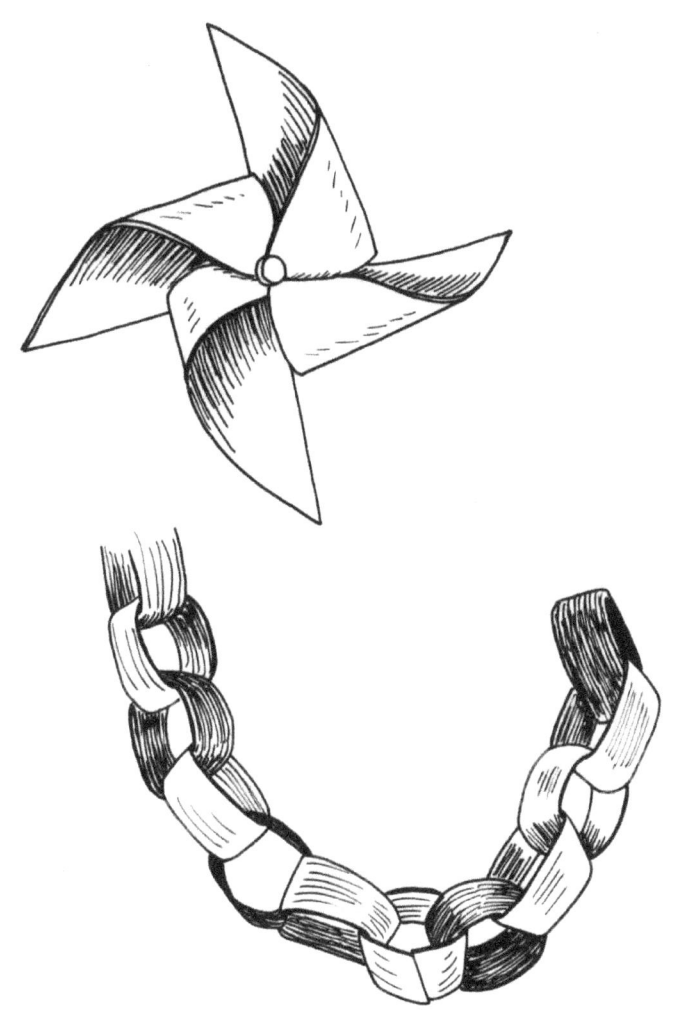

tale thirty

My eighth year of school was a fiasco that started when our local schoolhouse was destroyed by fire.

The gymnasium was spared, so the grammar school kids would attend classes there.

> But what was to happen to us high-schoolers, no one seemed to know.

> When we finally got the news, we couldn't believe it was so!

We were about to get an early dose of "bussing," it was pretty clear.

For nearly a mile each day I went on foot to our little country store,

Where I'd park myself beside some of my classmates for a half-hour or more,

    Until a big yellow school bus would arrive.

    And we would get aboard and off it would drive.

We soon began to realize just what we were in for!

The bus took us through the country picking up kids here and there.

Eventually they (but not us!) were unloaded at some school, somewhere.

> We were told it wasn't our school because of the "district" it was in.

> And another trip to pick up more children did then begin.

After taking that load back to the same school, we continued for about twelve miles to the County High School to begin our school year.

At the end of each school day, our path back home would be the same.

I didn't mind too much during the Fall months, but then Winter came –

> And I'd be leaving home before the break of day.

> Daddy had to get me a kerosene lantern to light my way.

But it was on one of those mornings that I witnessed something that my memory will always retain!

As I was heading out the door that day, expecting to see the night,

I saw instead a sky filled with dazzling colors and bright light!

> I was so scared, and I ran back inside screaming, "Daddy, the world is coming to an end!"
>
> He took one look outside and exclaimed: "No, that's an aurora borealis, my little friend,

And you may never see this again in your lifetime." And he was probably right.

At the end of that school year, my oldest sister intervened.

She had come up with a new plan for me, it seemed.

> She had contacted a boarding school, whose founder was a family friend,
>
> And made all the necessary arrangements for me to attend.

SHE HAD ENROLLED ME IN THE MARTHA BERRY SCHOOL FOR GIRLS WHERE FOR THREE HAPPY YEARS, I WOULD REMAIN! (<u>THE END</u>)

addendum

Other poems written by me
for special people and occasions

HAPPY BIRTHDAY JACKIE
(My very first limerick - April, 2013)

I have a dear sister named Jackie.
She's not too serious, but not whacky.
   She's sweet and demure,
   And lovable, for sure.
She's quite talkative, but never yakky!

She's celebrating her birthday today,
How old she is, she won't say.
   But I do know one thing...
   She's younger than Spring,
And will always remain that way!

A MARRIAGE
(May, 2013)

To Christina and Daniel on your wedding day...
May all the best in life come your way.

   May happiness reign supreme;
   May you fulfill every dream;

And may you always love each other, come what may!

ON VETERANS DAY
(May, 2013)

Oft times when life is moving so fast,
We tend to forget too much of our past.

   So let's pause a moment to recall
   Our most important people of all:

Those who served our country to make our freedom last!

(published by Eber & Wein - August, 2015. Book entitled "Beyond the Sea – Homecoming," page 11)

A BIRTHDAY IN NEW ORLEANS
(September 21, 2013)

My very special niece named
Hunter Louise
(whom I have loved for sixty years
without cease)
   Is celebrating her birthday today –

   A good reason to be in New Orleans,
   I say!

So Mr. Bartender, a bottle of champagne,
please!

2013 CHRISTMAS CARD
(December, 2013)

To my dearest friends both far and near,
'Tis once again that time of year,
   To wish you well in every way,
   To let you know I'm A-okay;

And to propose a toast to the coming
year — Hear! Hear!

MY PERIODONTIST
(June, 2014)

I have a periodontist named Jolene,
Who's the sweetest thing you've ever seen.

   But when she works,
   it kinda hurts –

But she's not trying to be mean!

THE FLORIDA PANHANDLE
(April, 2015)

Balmy breezes blow; blue-green
waters flow;
The soft, sandy beaches appear as snow.

   The skies are the bluest,
   the clouds the whitest;

   The sun above is always
   the brightest,

In "The Panhandle" that I know!

THE ARTIST
(May, 2015)

I have a cherished friend named John,
Who lives on a desert in Oregon.

   With camera in hand and
   his dog by his side,

   He roams the land, both
   far and wide.

And then, with paints and brush in
hand, he makes that land his own.

ELEGY WRITTEN FOR JACKIE
(December, 2015)

She walked in beauty and grace,
With the sweetest, smiling face.

   Oh, how she was loved by all,

   And was always at their
   beck and call.

And now there's no one left to take
her place.

POEM FOR JOHN
(May, 2016)

I employ a financial wizard named John,
Whose acumen I wholely depend upon;

    Without such, my pennies might all be gone,

    And I'd be up that preverbial tree alone.

But my piggy bank still rattles, so for now we've won.

2016 CHRISTMAS CARD
(December, 2016)

I raised my glass of champagne and wished everyone good cheer;

Sent Valentines to my loved ones both far and near;

    Carefully put away my Easter bonnet in mothballs;

    Stuffed myself with turkey, then hit all the shopping malls.

And now 'tis time for me to wish you Merry Christmas and a Very Happy New Year!

A VISIT FROM FRANK & HUNTER
(August, 2017)

Last evening I realized once again what a fortunate Aunt I am,

When a favorite niece and nephew came to visit from Alabam.

    Homemade maranara sauce they brought with two bottles of wine,

    And with pasta, greens and bread did we joyusly dine!

But the special part of the evening was the love that flowed like water over Hoover Dam!

2017 CHRISTMAS CARD
(December, 2017)

2017! Where, oh where, did it go?
Does anyone out there happen to know?

   I hear it's being replaced by a
   brand new year,

   Called "2018", that will soon
   be here.

Perhaps Santa's bringing it on his sleigh,
Ho! Ho! Ho!

PAM'S VISIT
(April, 2018)

At last my niece has come,
All the way from Oregon!

   A whole week will she be with me,
   And so very happy shall I be!

Until the day she must go home!!!!!

REMEMBERING 1940
(May, 2018)

Since today is May First, Two Thousand Eighteen,

It must be the birth date of my sister, Sandra Jean!

   I was only eight years old
   when first we met,

   But 'twas a day that I shall
   ne'er forget.

Because of the big black car she came in!!

www.ingramcontent.com/pod-product-compliance
Lightning Source LLC
Chambersburg PA
CBHW021954090426
42811CB00001B/29